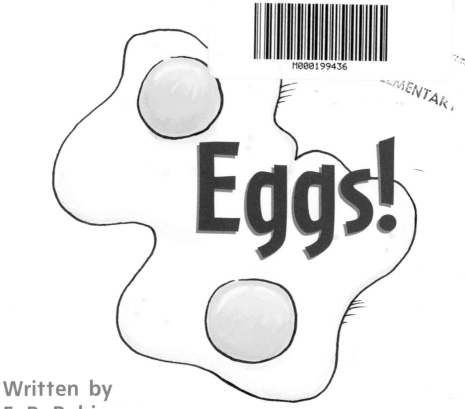

Eggs!

Written by
F. R. Robinson

Illustrated by
Randy Verougstraete

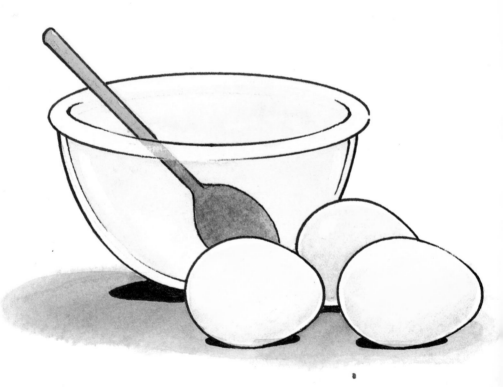

Look at the eggs.

Look at the man.

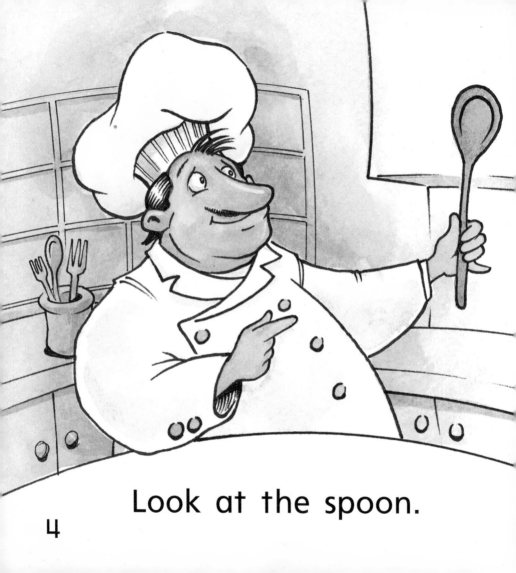

Look at the spoon.

4

Look at the pan.

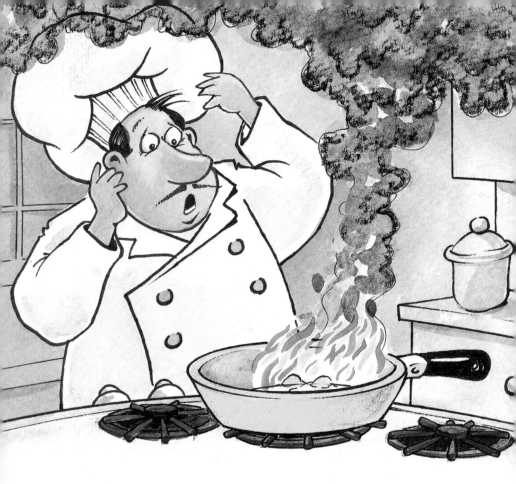

Look at the smoke.

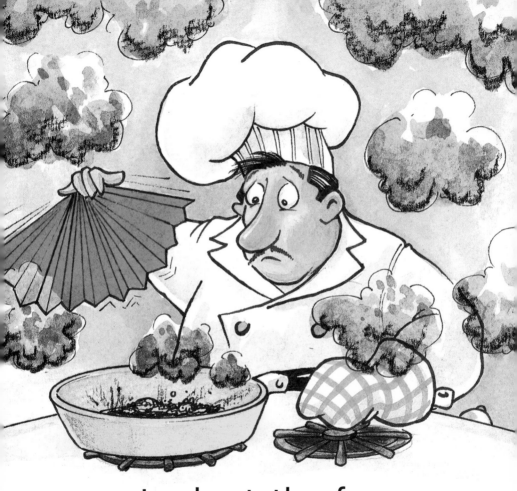

Look at the fan.

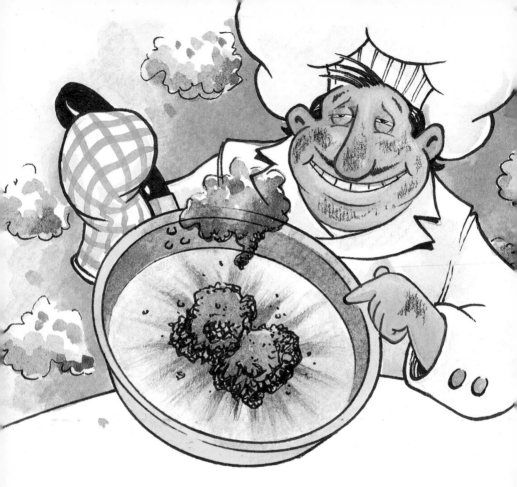

Look at the eggs!